ACTIVITY BOOK 3

Welcome to Our World

SECOND EDITION

Series Editors
Joan Kang Shin & JoAnn (Jodi) Crandall

NATIONAL GEOGRAPHIC LEARNING

Australia • Brazil • Canada • Mexico • Singapore • United Kingdom • United States

LET'S SHARE!

Listen and circle. **TR: AB.0.1**

1 2

Listen and color. Say. **TR: AB.0.2**

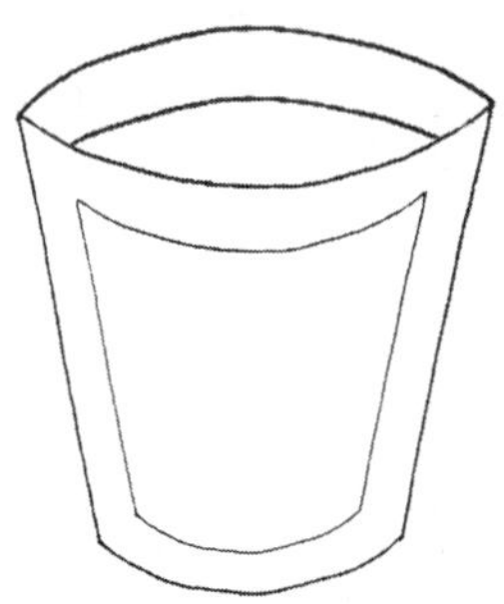

Listen and circle. **TR: AB.0.3**

1 2

Listen and color. **TR: AB.0.4**

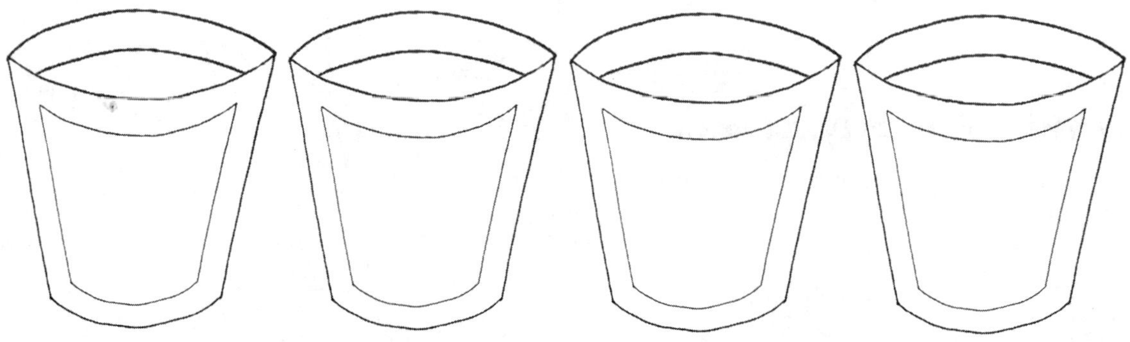

1 STAND UP, SIT DOWN

VOCABULARY Listen and point. Trace. **TR: AB.1.1**

SONG Listen and circle. **TR: AB.1.2**

THE SOUNDS OF ENGLISH Listen and say. Circle. **TR: AB.1.3**

  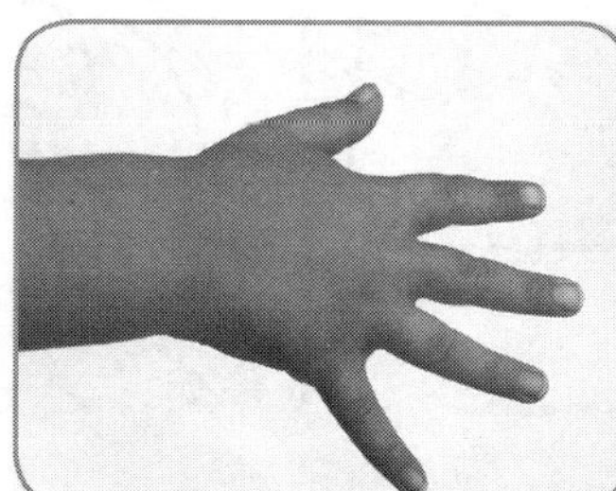  

CONCEPTS Count and say. Draw.

△ △ + △ = △ △ △

○ ○ ○ + ○ = ○ ○ ○ ○

□ + □ =

LANGUAGE IN USE

Listen and circle. **TR: AB.1.4**

1
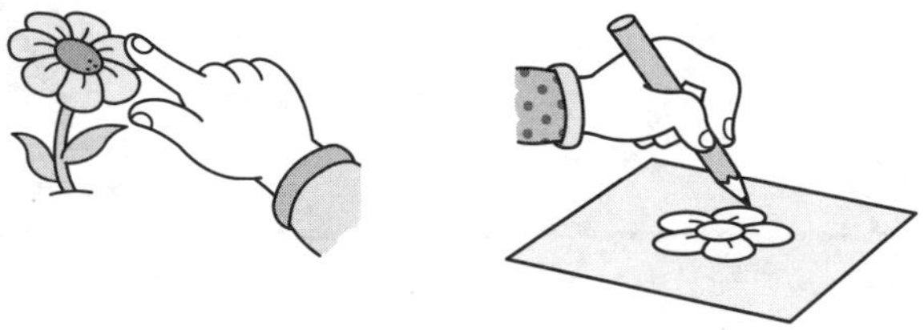

2

3

4

Listen. Draw and say. **TR: AB.1.5**

2 IT'S RAINING

VOCABULARY Draw a line and say.

SONG Listen and draw a line. **TR: AB.2.1**

1 2 3 4 5

THE SOUNDS OF ENGLISH Listen and say. Circle. **TR: AB.2.2**

CONCEPTS Listen and circle. **TR: AB.2.3**

LANGUAGE IN USE

Listen and circle. **TR: AB.2.4**

1

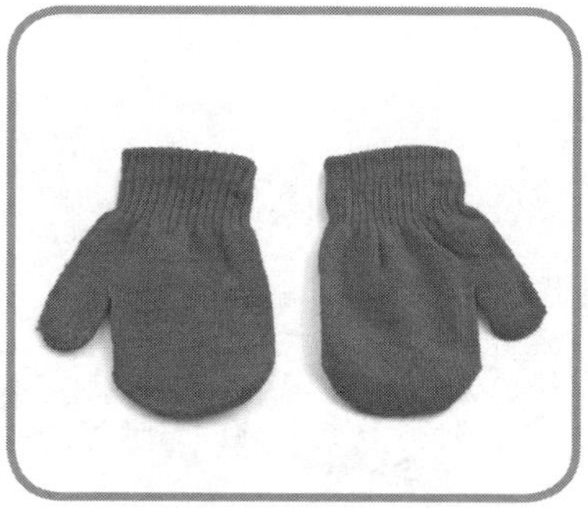

2

3

Listen. Draw and say. **TR: AB.2.5**

3 WILD ANIMALS

VOCABULARY Find and say.

SONG Listen. Draw lines. **TR: AB.3.1**

THE SOUNDS OF ENGLISH Listen and say. Circle. **TR: AB.3.2**

CONCEPTS Draw and say.

LANGUAGE IN USE

Listen and circle. **TR: AB.3.3**

1 

2 

3 

4 

Listen. Draw and say. **TR: AB.3.4**

4 SINGING AND DANCING

VOCABULARY Look and say. Circle.

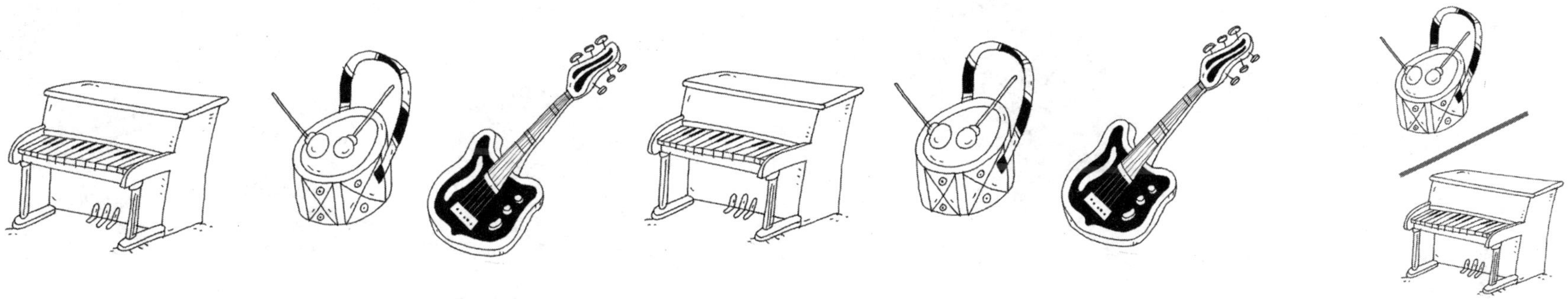

SONG Listen. Circle. **TR: AB.4.1**

1

2

THE SOUNDS OF ENGLISH Listen and say. Circle. **TR: AB.4.2**

CONCEPTS Draw a line and say.

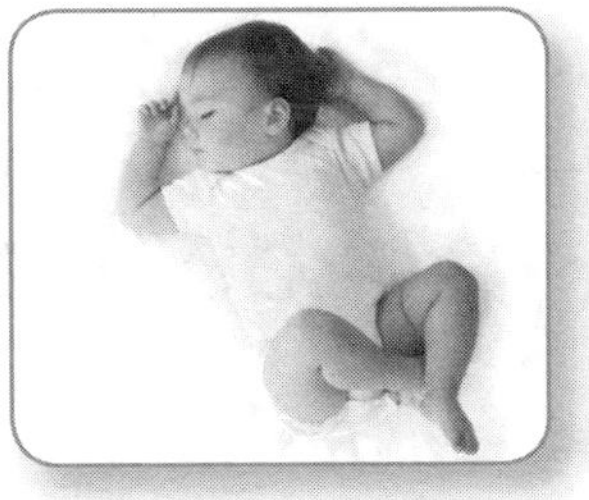

LANGUAGE IN USE

Listen and circle. **TR: AB.4.3**

1

2

3

4

Listen. Draw and say. **TR: AB.4.4**

REVIEW

Listen and circle. **TR: AB.4.6**

Draw a line and say.

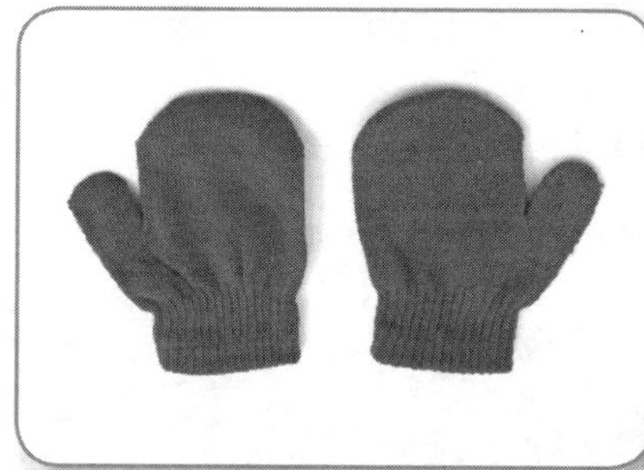

Listen and say. **TR: AB.4.7**

5 SEE, SMELL, HEAR

VOCABULARY Listen and draw a line. Say. **TR: AB.5.1**

SONG Listen and circle. **TR: AB.5.2**

THE SOUNDS OF ENGLISH Listen and say. Circle. **TR: AB.5.3**

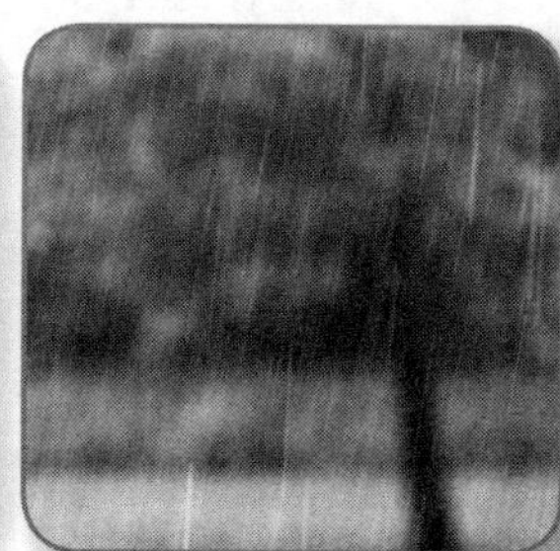

CONCEPTS Listen and draw a line. Draw and say. **TR: AB.5.4**

LANGUAGE IN USE

Listen and circle. **TR: AB.5.5**

1  

2  

3  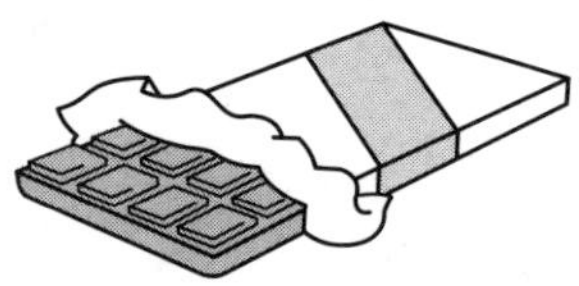

4  

Listen. Draw and say. **TR: AB.5.6**

6 STORY TIME

VOCABULARY Say and circle.

SONG Listen and circle. **TR: AB.6.1**

THE SOUNDS OF ENGLISH Listen and say. Circle. **TR: AB.6.2**

CONCEPTS Circle the number.

1 2 3

1 (2) 3

1 2 3

1 2 3

1 2 3

1 2 3

LANGUAGE IN USE

Listen and circle. **TR: AB.6.3**

1 

2 

3 

4 

Listen. Draw and say. **TR: AB.6.4**

7 IT'S A PARTY!

VOCABULARY Draw. Say.

SONG Listen and circle. **TR: AB.7.1**

THE SOUNDS OF ENGLISH Listen and say. Circle. **TR: AB.7.2**

CONCEPTS Draw.

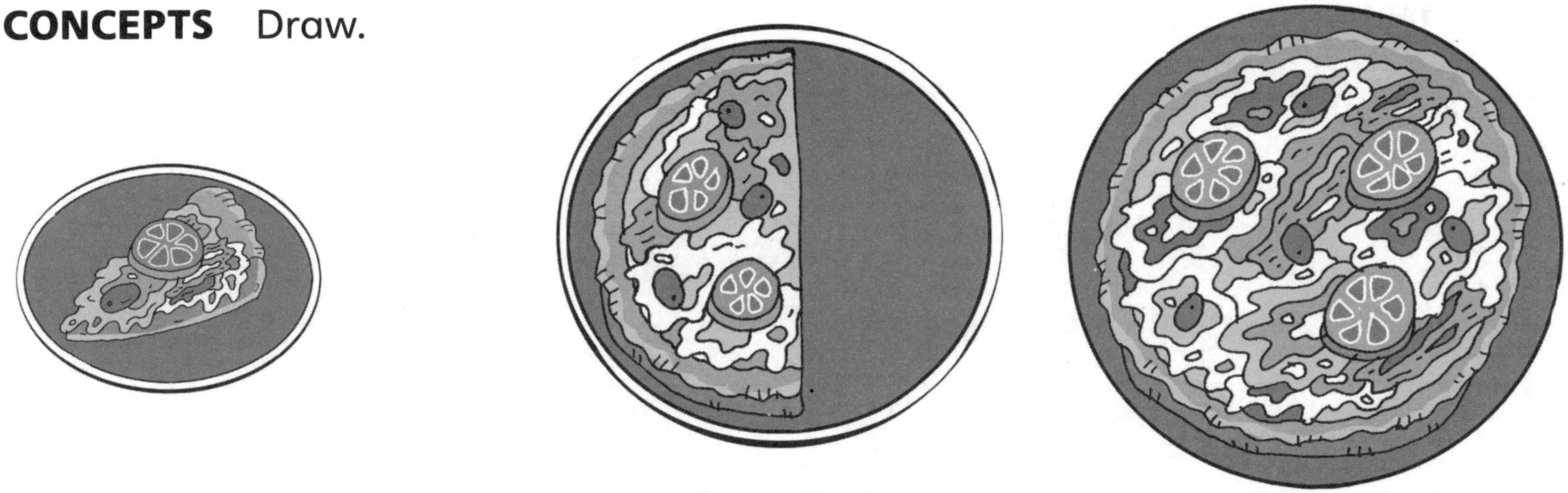

LESS

MORE

LANGUAGE IN USE

Listen and circle. **TR: AB.7.3**

Listen. Color and say. **TR: AB.7.4**

8 OUR WORLD

VOCABULARY Listen and draw a line. **TR: AB.8.1**

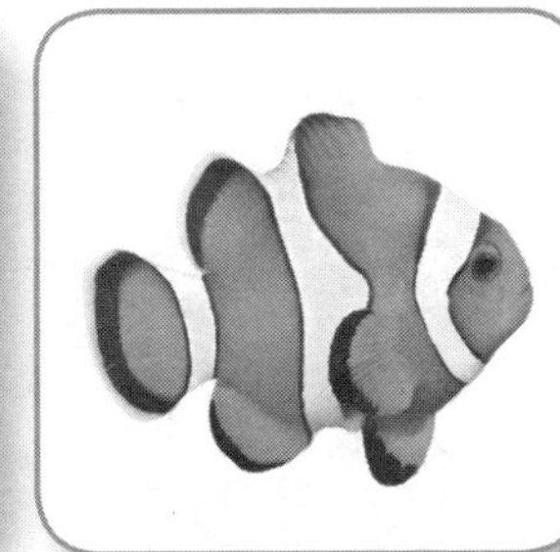

SONG Listen. Draw a line. **TR: AB.8.2**

THE SOUNDS OF ENGLISH Listen and say. Circle. **TR: AB.8.3**

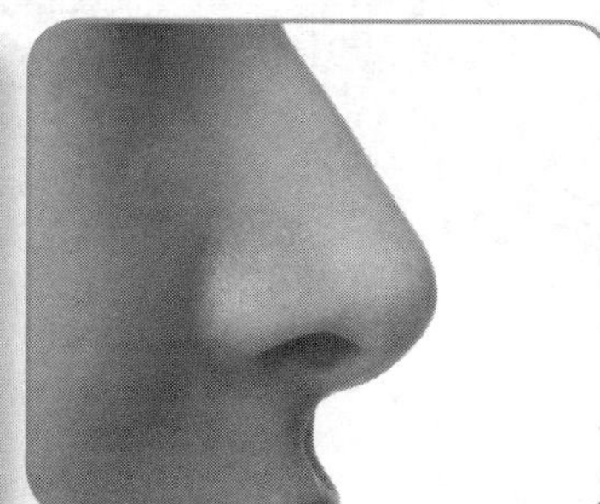

CONCEPTS Listen and draw a line. **TR: AB.8.4**

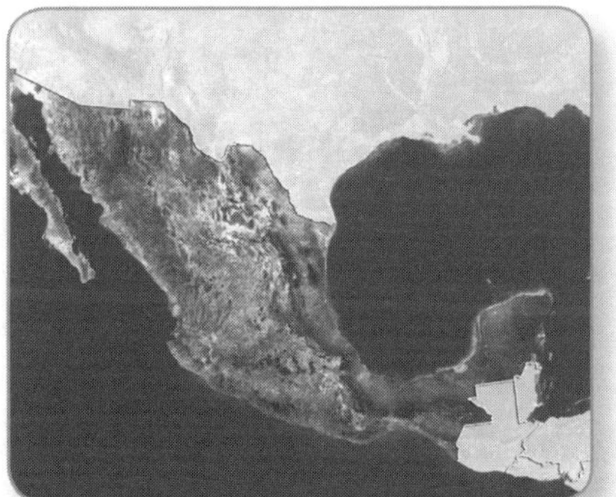

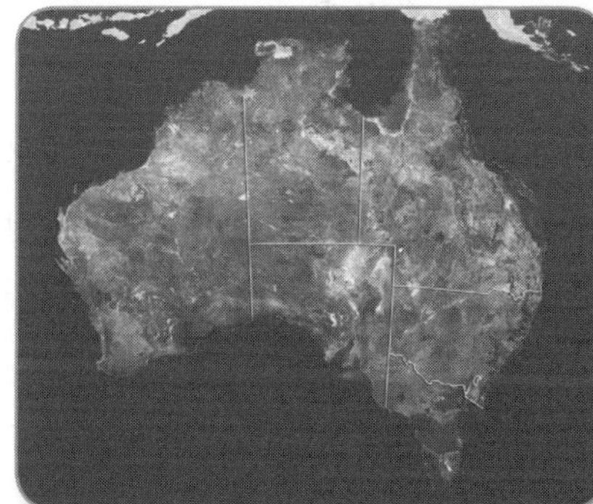

LANGUAGE IN USE

Listen and draw a line. **TR: AB.8.5**

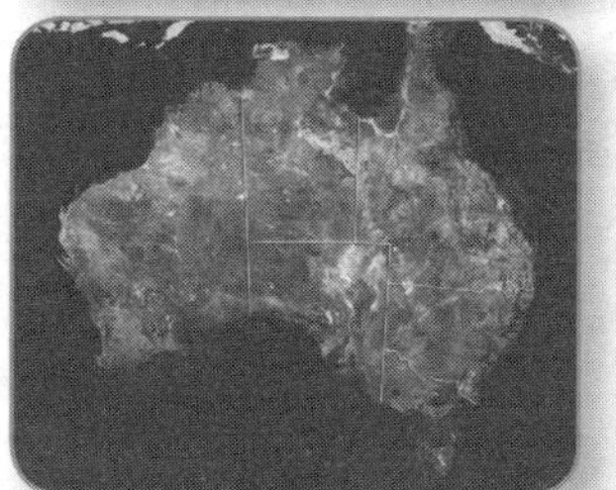

Listen. Draw and say. **TR: AB.8.6**

REVIEW

Listen and color. **TR: AB.8.8**

Listen and draw a line. **TR: AB.8.9**

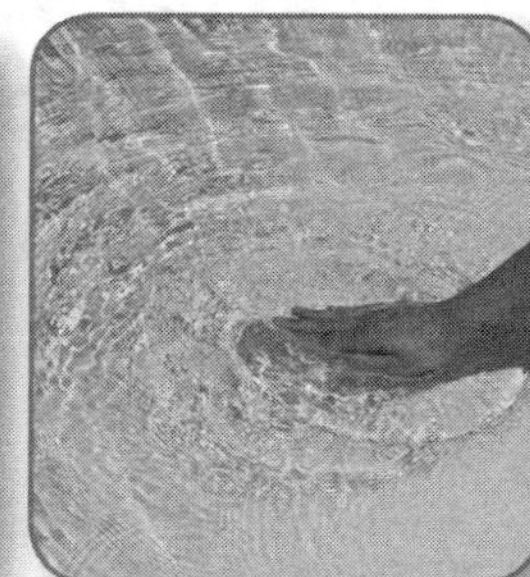

WRITING Listen and say. Trace and write. **TR: AB.ABC1** Use with Unit I.

A A A

A A A

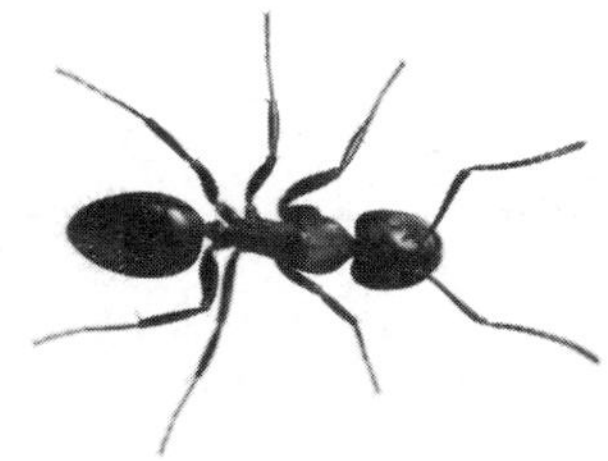

ANT

B B B

B B B

BUS

WRITING Listen and say. Trace and write. **TR: AB.ABC2**

Use with Unit I.

C C C

c c c

CAR

I I I

2 2 2

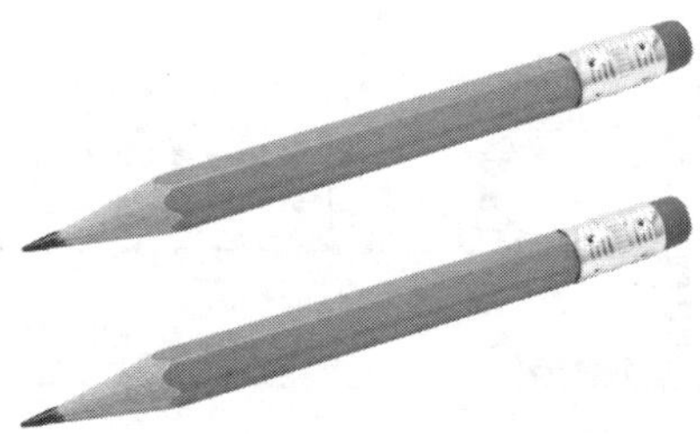

WRITING Listen and say. Trace and write. **TR: AB.ABC3**

Use with Unit 2.

D D D

D D D

DUCK

E E E

E E E

EGG

WRITING Listen and say. Trace and write. **TR: AB.ABC4**

Use with Unit 2.

F F F

F F F

3 3 3

4 4 4

FIRE TRUCK

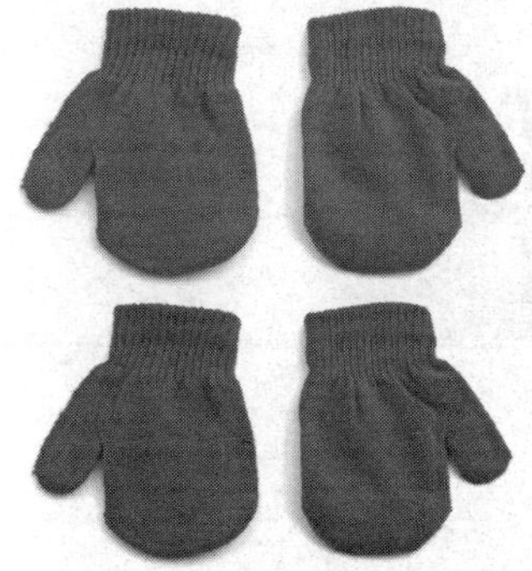

WRITING Listen and say. Trace and write. **TR: AB.ABC5** Use with Unit 3.

G G G

G G G

GOAT

H H H

H H H

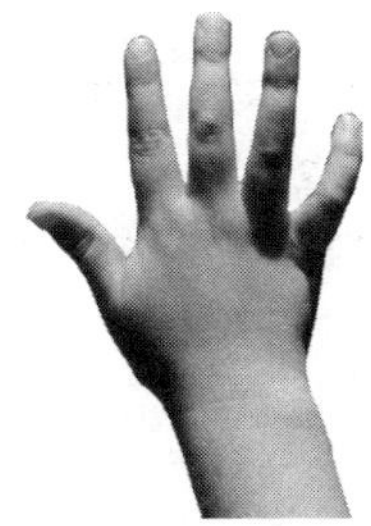

HAND

WRITING Listen and say. Trace and write. **TR: AB.ABC6**

Use with Unit 3.

I I I

I I I

5 5 5

6 6 6

ICE CREAM

WRITING Listen and say. Trace and write. TR: AB.ABC7 Use with Unit 4.

J J J

J J J

K K K

K K K

JUICE

KING

WRITING Listen and say. Trace and write. **TR: AB.ABC8**

Use with Unit 4.

L L L

LION

L L L

7 7 7

8 8 8

WRITING Listen and say. Trace and write. **TR: AB.ABC9**

Use with Unit 5.

M M M

M M M

N N N

N N N

MILK

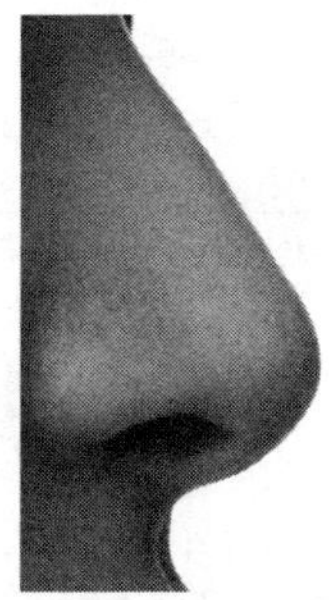

NOSE

WRITING Listen and say. Trace and write. **TR: AB.ABC10** Use with Unit 5.

O O O

O O O

ORANGE

9 9 9

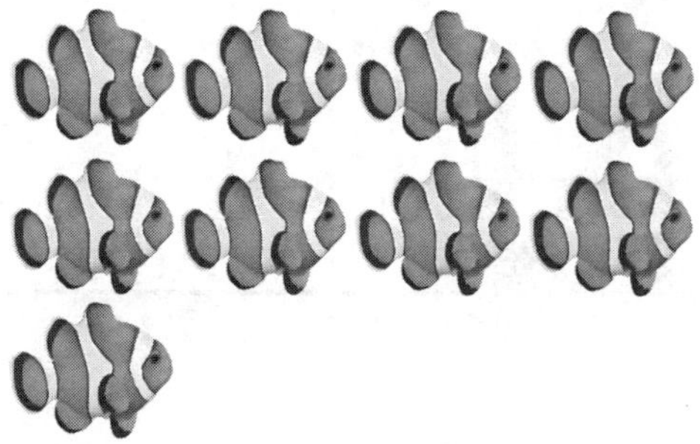

10 10 10

WRITING Listen and say. Trace and write. **TR: AB.ABC11**

Use with Unit 6.

P P P

P P P

Q Q Q

Q Q Q

PUZZLE

QUEEN

WRITING Listen and say. Trace and write. TR: AB.ABC12

Use with Unit 6.

R R R

R R R

RABBIT

S S S

S S S

SOCKS

WRITING Listen and say. Trace and write. **TR: AB.ABC13** Use with Unit 7.

T T T

T T T

TRAIN

U U U

U U U

UMBRELLA

WRITING Listen and say. Trace and write. TR: AB.ABC14

Use with Unit 7.

V V V

V V V

VIOLIN

W W W

W W W

WINDOW

WRITING Listen and say. Trace and write. **TR: AB.ABC15**

Use with Unit 8.

X X X

X X X

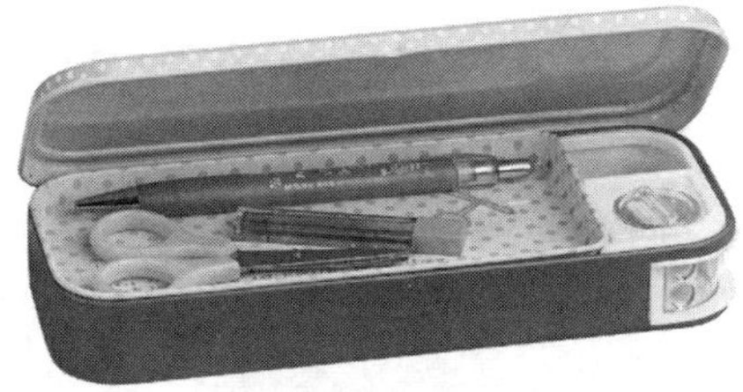

BOX

Y Y Y

Y Y Y

YOGURT

WRITING Listen and say. Trace and write. **TR: AB.ABC16**

Use with Unit 8.

Z Z Z

z z z

ZEBRA

MY NAME IS

UNIT 1

REVIEW Do it!

TOUCH

READ

WRITE

COLOR

SIT DOWN

STAND UP

DRAW

COUNT

UNIT 2

REVIEW Count and say.

UNIT 3

REVIEW Look and say. Draw.

UNIT 4

REVIEW Listen and color. **TR: AB.4.5**

UNIT 5

REVIEW Point and say. Circle.

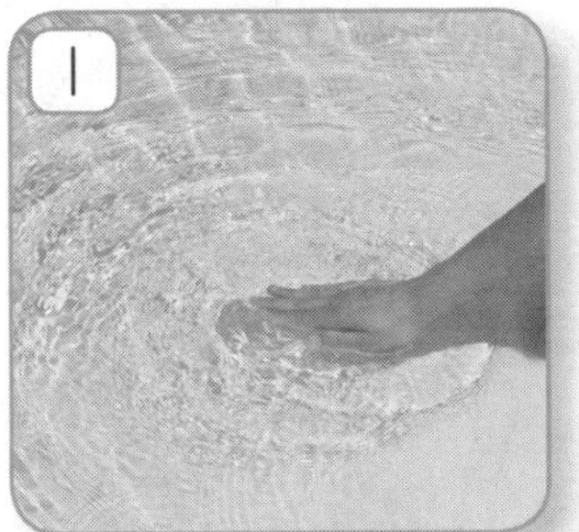

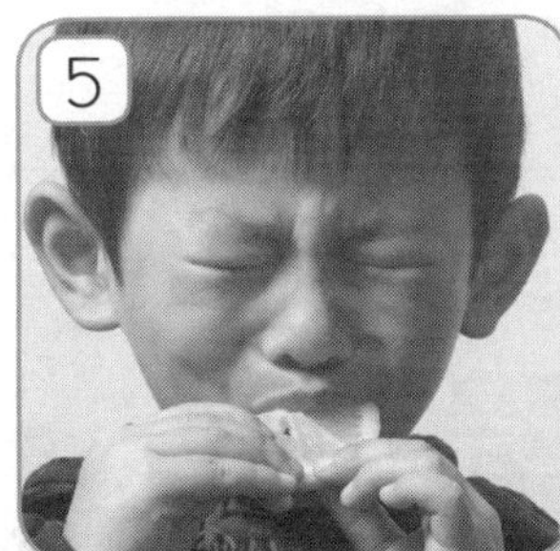

UNIT 6

REVIEW Look and say.

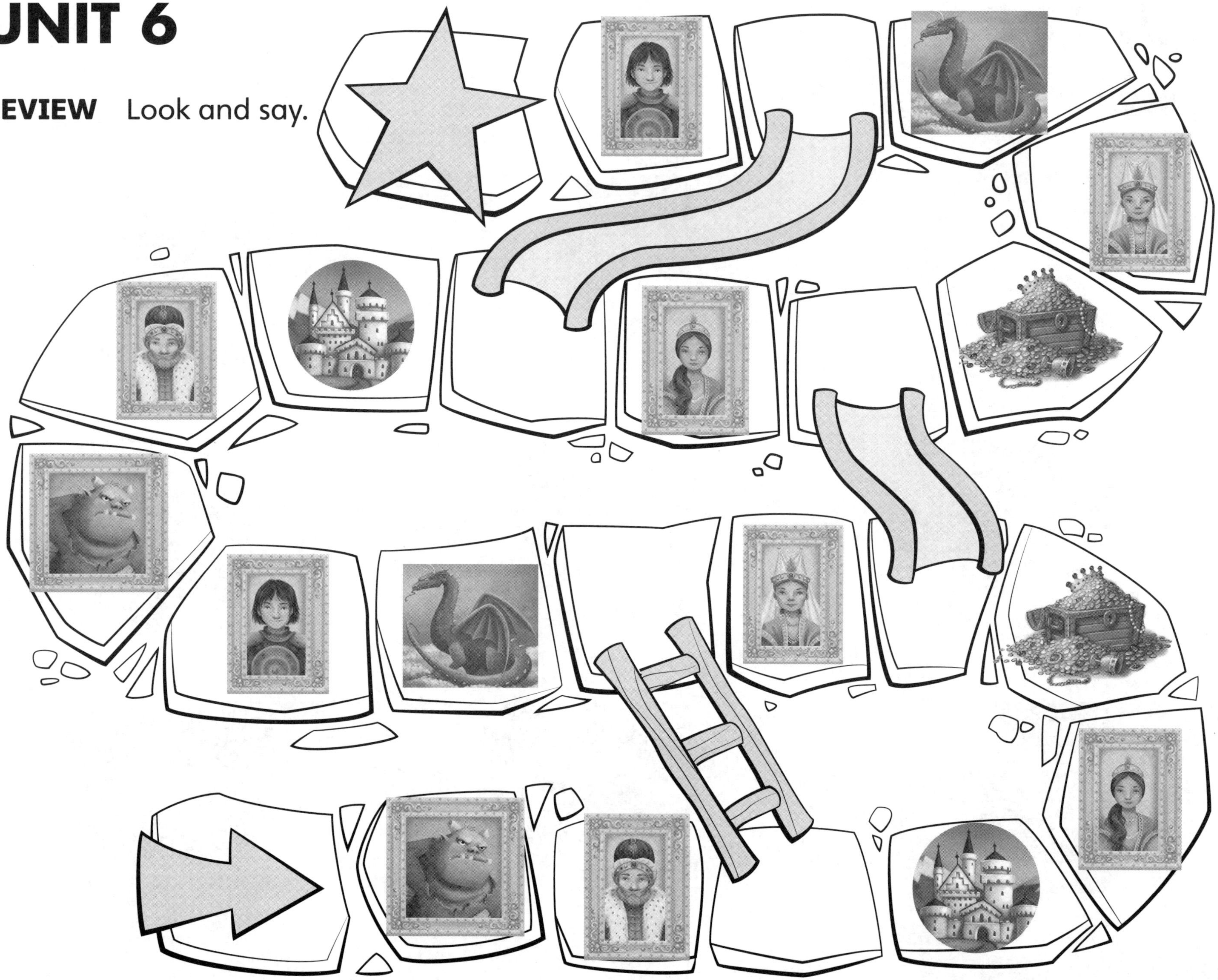

UNIT 7

REVIEW Find and draw. Color.

UNIT 8

REVIEW Listen and draw. **TR: AB.8.7**